OPHIUCHUS

Ras Alhague

Ras Algethi

HERCULES

CORONA
Gemma   Borealis

DRACO

BOOTES

Arcturus

Cor Caroli

LIBRA

Zuben el Chamali

Zuben el Genubi

Vindemiatrix

Albireo

CYGNI

LYRA

Vega

OUT OF THIS WORLD

POEMS AND FACTS ABOUT SPACE

BY AMY E. SKLANSKY

ILLUSTRATED BY STACEY SCHUETT

ALFRED A. KNOPF NEW YORK

COUNTDOWN

T-minus: 10

9

8

Seat belt tightening.

7

6

Knuckles whitening.

5

4

Rockets roaring.

3

2

1

Spaceship soaring!

Fact: In order to reach space, a spaceship has to go really fast to break free from the powerful pull of Earth's gravity. When fuel is ignited inside a rocket, gases (and fire!) shoot out from the bottom of the rocket, pushing it upward. For example, the rockets that propelled the space shuttle helped it reach 17,500 miles (28,000 kilometers) per hour, or about 250 times faster than the speed limit on most highways.

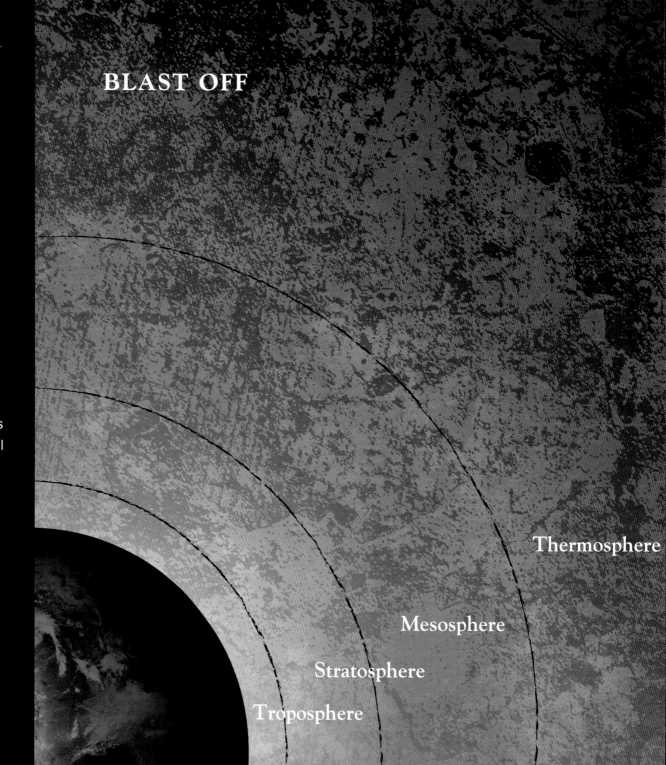

BLAST OFF

Fact: There are five layers of atmosphere between Earth and outer space. The layer closest to Earth is called the troposphere. This layer extends 6 to 9 miles (10 to 14 kilometers) in the sky and is where most of our weather occurs. On top of that is the stratosphere, where airplanes usually fly. The stratosphere is also home to the ozone layer. Meteors burn up in the air of the mesosphere. The thermosphere is the layer in which the International Space Station circles the Earth. Most satellites orbit the Earth in the thermosphere and also the exosphere, the final layer of atmosphere before space. The exosphere ends and outer space begins at about 6,200 miles (10,000 kilometers) from the surface of the Earth. It took the space shuttle about 8½ minutes from launch to reach its orbit in the thermosphere.

Thermosphere

Mesosphere

Stratosphere

Troposphere

AFTER BLASTOFF

The Earth
fills
their window

and then
drops away,
like a

       basketball

          baseball

            golfball

              marble.

How far from home
they've traveled today.

Fact: America's *Apollo 11* mission was the first to put humans on the Moon. It took less than 4½ days to travel the 244,391 miles (393,309 kilometers) to get there. While Michael Collins piloted the *Apollo* in orbit around the Moon, Neil Armstrong and Buzz Aldrin landed in a lunar module and walked around on the dusty surface conducting experiments.

Fact: Earth's gravity is the force that pulls objects toward its center. When astronauts are in orbit, they experience very little gravity (most call this zero gravity), which gives them a feeling of weightlessness or floating. This lack of gravity means that they can stand horizontally on a wall and that objects, even their meals, must be fastened down or they will float free. Astronauts must hold on to straps or handles with their hands and feet as they move. They sleep zipped into sleeping bags that are fastened to a wall or the ceiling, so they don't float around.

ZERO GRAVITY

In zero gravity
you can sleep

on the ceiling.

Zero gravity
must be

an odd feeling.

WEIGHTLESS WONDER

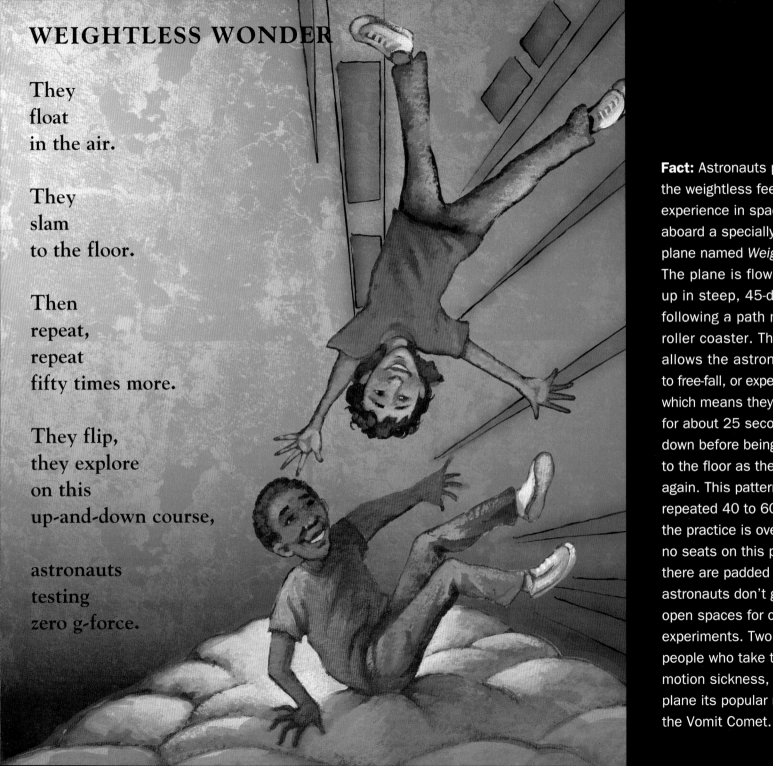

They
float
in the air.

They
slam
to the floor.

Then
repeat,
repeat
fifty times more.

They flip,
they explore
on this
up-and-down course,

astronauts
testing
zero g-force.

Fact: Astronauts prepare for the weightless feeling they will experience in space by riding aboard a specially outfitted plane named *Weightless Wonder.* The plane is flown down and up in steep, 45-degree arcs, following a path much like a roller coaster. This flight path allows the astronauts-in-training to free-fall, or experience 0 g-force, which means they float in the air for about 25 seconds on the way down before being thrust back to the floor as the plane climbs again. This pattern is typically repeated 40 to 60 times before the practice is over. There are no seats on this plane; instead, there are padded floors so the astronauts don't get hurt, and open spaces for conducting experiments. Two out of three people who take this ride get motion sickness, earning the plane its popular nickname—the Vomit Comet.

The suit deflects
as it protects
from any injury.

Good work is done
in shade or sun,
though movement does lack grace.

No astronaut
is ever caught
without a suit in space.

Fact: Once astronauts reach space or the space station, they typically remove their suits and wear regular clothes, since they are inside a carefully controlled environment. However, they must suit up to go outside the spaceship. A space suit provides protection from the extreme temperatures in space, which range from hundreds of degrees above zero in sunlight to hundreds of degrees below zero in shadow. The suit also protects astronauts from solar radiation, glare, and micrometeoroids (small particles traveling through space), which could otherwise harm them. In space, there is no atmosphere, no air to breathe, so an astronaut carries an 8-hour supply of oxygen in a tank. Because working in a space suit is quite awkward (it weighs about 280 pounds on Earth and takes about 45 minutes to put on), astronauts practice space walks here on Earth by suiting up and performing tasks underwater in a huge pool. A space suit has so many different features that it is very expensive to produce: each costs more than $10 million.

PACKING FOR THE MOON

Neil Armstrong packed
    music recorded by his wife
    a propeller fragment from
       the Wright brothers' flyer
    mint Life Savers
    and a comb.

Buzz Aldrin packed
    his mother's lucky charm bracelet
    four gold olive branches
    a vial of wine
    and a wafer.

Michael Collins packed
    poems and prayers
    coins, cuff links, tiepins, rings
    and a small lucky charm holding
       fifty tiny ivory elephants.

What
    would *you* pack?

Fact: Each astronaut on the *Apollo 11* mission to the Moon was allowed to pack one Personal Preference Kit (or PPK), with personal items for the journey. The PPK was a small bag made of white fiberglass cloth, measuring 2 inches by 4 inches by 8 inches (a bit larger than a box of Girl Scout cookies).

The propeller fragment Neil Armstrong packed was from the engine-powered flyer built and flown by Wilbur and Orville Wright in the first successful manned flight, on December 17, 1903. Buzz Aldrin brought wine and a wafer so he could celebrate Holy Communion, his way of giving thanks. One of four gold olive branches was left on the Moon as a symbol of peace. The others were brought back to Earth and presented to each of the astronauts' wives. Michael Collins packed lots of small items to give away as gifts when he returned to Earth.

MOON

Marvelous
Opaque
Orb.
Night-light
    for the world.

Fact: The Moon does not generate its own light. It reflects light from the Sun. Like the Sun, the Moon rises in the east and sets in the west. Each day it rises about 50 minutes later than the day before.

LEFT BEHIND

Astronaut footprints
mark the Moon's dusty surface,
lasting mementos.

Fact: The surface of the Moon is covered with regolith, a mixture of fine dust and rock particles created by meteor impacts. Because there is no weather or air on the Moon, the footprints made by astronauts will likely remain unchanged on its surface for billions of years. Twelve men have walked (and left their mark) on the Moon—the first on July 20, 1969, and the last on December 14, 1972.

Fact: The first artificial satellite, *Sputnik 1,* was launched by the Soviet Union in 1957. It was the size of a large beach ball, though it weighed about 184 pounds (83 kilograms). It zoomed around the Earth about every 96 minutes. Today, satellites come in many shapes and sizes and perform a wide variety of functions, including weather prediction; navigation and mapmaking; communication transmission for television, Internet, and cell phones; and spying and other military uses. As of 2011, more than 3,500 satellites were in orbit around the Earth. Their altitudes ranged from about 100 to 22,000 miles (160 to 35,400 kilometers).

SATELLITES

Satellites circle
round and round,
bouncing signals
from the ground.

Stars no longer
guide at night;
we plot our course
by satellite.

Orbiting Earth
in the thermosphere;
making phone calls
loud and clear;

Sending TV
overseas;
helping surf the Web
with ease.

Satellites circle
round and round,
tracing Earth
without a sound.

WISH UPON A . . .

My brother wished
upon a star
racing 'cross the sky.

"It won't come true,"
I said to him.
"And here's the reason why:

That streak was not
a star at all.
It was a meteor.

Don't hold your breath,
you won't collect
whatever you wished for."

Turned out I'd made
a big mistake,
correct though I might be—

For then my brother
walked away
and would not play with me.

Fact: Meteoroids are bits of rock and metal floating in space. Most are the size of a grain of salt, but they can be larger than a boulder. If a meteoroid enters the Earth's atmosphere, it burns up, creating a bright streak in the sky called a meteor. When a meteor hits the Earth, it is called a meteorite and looks like a rock.

In August, you can watch the night sky for the Perseids, one of the most brilliant annual meteor showers. If you look toward the constellation Perseus at the peak of this meteor shower, you might see 50 to 80 meteors every hour.

COMET

Dirty ball of snow
Set ablaze by our own Sun.
Its tail streaks the sky.

Fact: A comet is a giant snowball of ice and dust that orbits the Sun. When a comet's orbit brings it close to the Sun, some of the outer parts melt, which leaves a bright streak (the "tail") in the sky, visible for weeks or even months. A comet's "head" may be a few miles across, but its gaseous tail can be millions of miles long and arc across a large part of the night sky. The most famous comet is named Halley's comet. It can be viewed from Earth every 76 years on average, which means its next appearance will be in 2061. You might look for it with your children or grandchildren!

Fact: A star begins as a giant cloud of gas. Over time, gravity pulls this material closer and closer together until the atoms are so charged that they begin to fuse, or stick to each other. This fusing, or fusion, creates tremendous amounts of energy. A star's color depends on how hot it is and the amount of energy it gives off. From hottest to coolest, stars can be colored blue, white, yellow, orange, or red. Stars don't actually twinkle. The movement of the air around the Earth creates the twinkling effect. If you saw a star from outer space, it would look like a steady dot of light.

TWINKLE

Twinkle, twinkle, little star.
Charged-up gas is what you are.
Yellow, blue, sometimes red.
Atoms fusing overhead.
Twinkle, twinkle, little star.
Shining at me from afar.

SUN

Hot dot

Far star

Fusion profusion

Sun

Fact: The surface of the Sun can be as hot as 10,000°F (5,500°C), and the core is many, many times hotter still, which is why we can feel the Sun's heat here on Earth. The Sun is the closest star to Earth, at 93 million miles (150 million kilometers) away. The next closest star is a whopping 25 trillion miles (40 trillion kilometers) away. Our Sun is about 870,000 miles (1.4 million kilometers) across, which makes it an average-sized star. Still, its size is enormous compared to Earth—more than 1.3 million Earths could fit inside the Sun!

HUNGRY MOON

Fact: The Moon orbits the Earth, and as it makes its way, we gradually see more or less of it depending on the position of the Sun. When the Sun and Moon are on opposite sides of the Earth, the Moon looks round and bright and is called a Full Moon. After that a bit less of the sunlit part of the Moon can be seen each night—this is called waning and makes it look as if the Moon is shrinking. When the Sun and Moon are on the same side of the Earth, the Moon looks invisible or dark and is called a New Moon. After that a bit more of the sunlit part of the Moon can be seen each night—this is called waxing and makes it look as if the Moon is growing. Every 29½ days, these lunar phases repeat.

Waxing Moon
eats the light,
growing larger
every night.

Hungry Moon
still wants more,
each night bigger
than before.

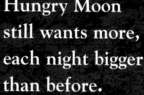

Well-fed Moon
now quite full . . .

then it feels
the darkness pull.

Waning Moon
loses glow.
Every night
its shadow grows.

Fading Moon
fills with dark;
no light, no beam,
no glow, no spark.

New Moon is
content tonight—
but soon begins
to eat the light.

I'm planning my vacation
somewhere far away.
But I'm not sure just where to go
on my next holiday.

It rarely rains on Mercury,
and I enjoy the Sun.
Then again, there's not much air,
and burning up's no fun!

On Venus, I could marvel
at a sunrise in the west.
Nice . . . except sulfuric clouds
do not encourage guests.

Facts: Crater-covered **Mercury** is the smallest planet and closest to the Sun. Its average daytime temperature can be as high as 800°F (427°C). Mercury has no permanent atmosphere, so there would be no air to breathe.

Venus is the easiest planet to spot; visible for a few hours after sunset or before sunrise, it often shines brighter than the brightest star. Venus's covering of thick sulfuric acid and its dense, mostly carbon dioxide atmosphere create a "greenhouse effect" and make the average surface temperature about 900°F (482°C). Most planets rotate in a counterclockwise direction; only Venus rotates clockwise, causing the Sun to rise in the west and set in the east.

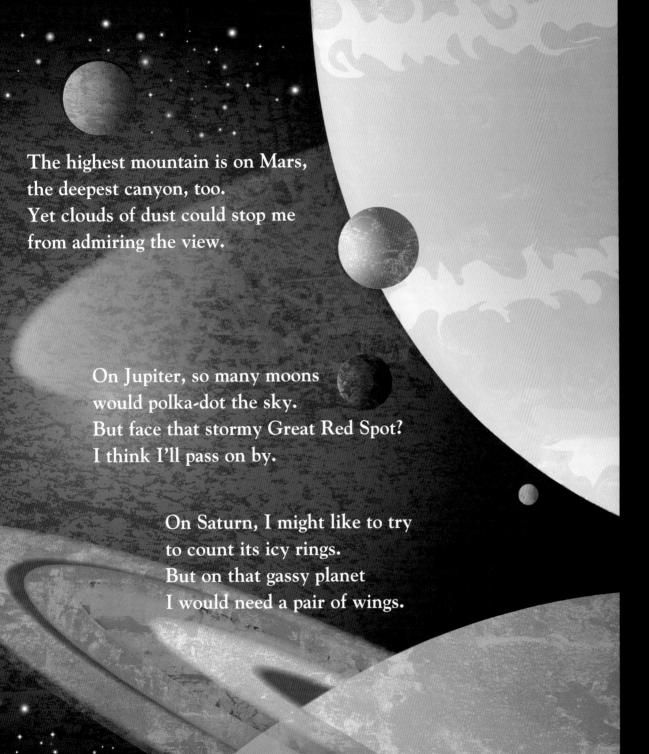

The highest mountain is on Mars,
the deepest canyon, too.
Yet clouds of dust could stop me
from admiring the view.

On Jupiter, so many moons
would polka-dot the sky.
But face that stormy Great Red Spot?
I think I'll pass on by.

On Saturn, I might like to try
to count its icy rings.
But on that gassy planet
I would need a pair of wings.

Mars is the most likely planet for manned space exploration. However, even a visit to "nearby" Mars from Earth would take about one year and eight months round-trip. Mars gets its reddish color from the rusty dust (iron oxide) that covers its surface. The highest mountain in our solar system, Olympus Mons (three times higher than Earth's Mount Everest), is found on Mars, as is the deepest system of canyons, far deeper than Earth's Grand Canyon.

Jupiter, the largest planet, is made up mostly of gaseous and liquid hydrogen. The Great Red Spot is a hurricane-like storm that has been raging for hundreds of years. Jupiter has more than sixty moons.

Saturn is circled by seven major rings, formed from thousands of narrow ringlets. The rings are made of ice, dust, and rocks that can be as small as a grain of sand or as big as a car. Saturn is made up of a small core of rock and ice wrapped in an outer gaseous layer, so its surface isn't solid like Earth's.

Uranus, toppled planet,
which rotates on its side,
just might make me woozy
like a wild amusement ride.

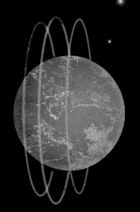

I like to feel a playful breeze
ruffle through my hair,
but the fast, fierce winds of Neptune
will keep me far from there.

The first planet to be discovered
by a telescope, **Uranus** spins on
its side. It was probably knocked
into this position by another
large body.

Neptune is the coldest planet in
the solar system, with an average
temperature of about –350°F
(–212°C), much colder than the
Earth's South Pole. It also has the
fastest winds, which can blow up to
about 730 miles (1,175 kilometers)
per hour.

Earth is the only planet known to
support life and to have water in all
three forms: solid, liquid, and gas.

I wouldn't have these problems
if I stayed right here on Earth.
Interplanetary travel
seems more trouble than it's worth.

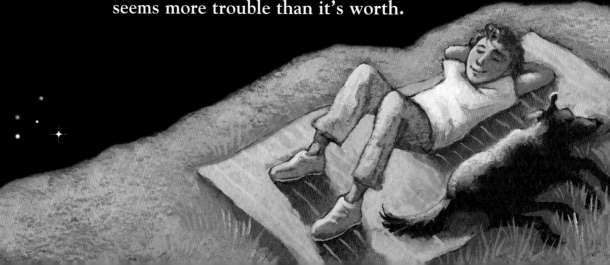

BLACK HOLE

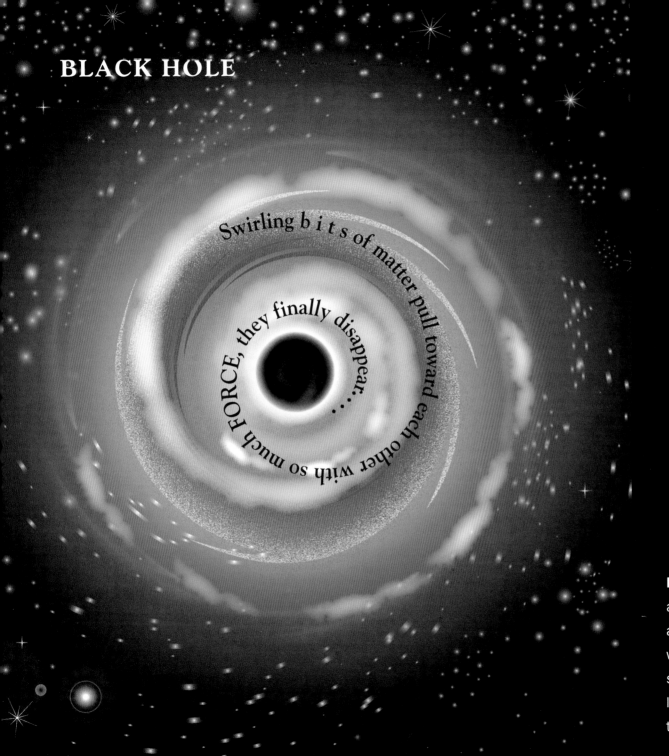

Swirling *b i t s* of matter pull toward each other with so much FORCE, they finally disappear. . . .

Fact: A black hole was once a massive star that exploded and then collapsed in on itself with great force. Its gravity is so strong that nothing, not even light, can escape, making it a truly black hole.

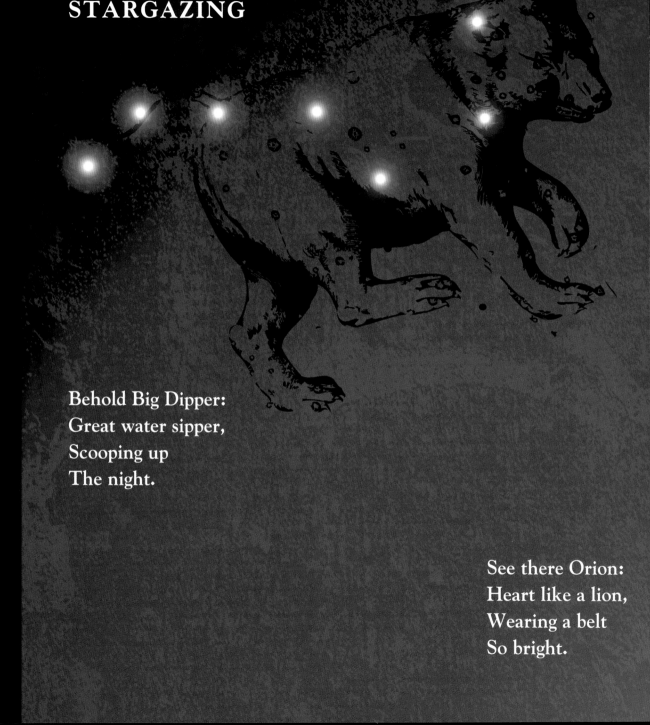

Fact: Over the centuries, people have used their imaginations to group stars into constellations, or configurations that resemble a person or object. Most of the constellations were inspired by Greek myths. Some constellations have different names and stories in different cultures. There are eighty-eight constellations officially recognized by astronomers. Because the Earth is constantly rotating and revolving, your view of the night sky and its constellations changes a little bit every night and is quite different from season to season.

Fact: The Big Dipper is a group of stars that seems to resemble a dipper or ladle. It is technically called an asterism, which is a recognizable pattern of stars that can be part of one or more constellations. The Big Dipper is part of the constellation Ursa Major (the Great Bear).

Behold Big Dipper:
Great water sipper,
Scooping up
The night.

See there Orion:
Heart like a lion,
Wearing a belt
So bright.

And look at these:
The Pleiades,
Scattered like doves
In flight.

Their stories are
From long ago,
So far away
Their light.

The stars are like
A storybook
Printed on
The night.

Fact: The three stars that form the belt of Orion, the brave hunter in Greek mythology, make this constellation easy to spot in the night sky. Orion is positioned near the celestial equator, which means it can be seen in both hemispheres. Myths tell us that Orion might be fighting Taurus, the Bull, or chasing Lepus, the Hare, across the heavens.

Fact: The Pleiades (pronounced *PLEE-uh-deez*) is a cluster of stars in the constellation Taurus that can be seen in the Northern Hemisphere in the winter months. In mythology, the Pleiades are seven sisters: nymphs in the service of the goddess Artemis. Some myths say that to save them from being chased by Orion, the Pleiades were turned into doves and later into stars.

MY PLACE

Universe

Galaxy

Solar System

Fact: Most scientists believe that the universe began about 13.7 billion years ago with a gigantic explosion called the Big Bang. A group of billions or even trillions of stars held together by gravity is called a galaxy. The universe contains billions of galaxies. Our spiral-shaped galaxy is called the Milky Way. A solar system is a collection of planets and other objects that orbit a star. Our solar system consists of the Sun, eight major planets, several dwarf planets, and many moons, asteroids, comets, and meteoroids.

Fact: So far we do not know of life existing on any other planet. However, people started studying the heavens with telescopes in the early 1600s. Since then, telescopes have become more advanced. In 1990, the United States put into orbit the giant Hubble Space Telescope, which made thousands of astronomical discoveries. For instance, we've glimpsed hundreds of planets orbiting other stars, as the Earth orbits the Sun. As technology improves even further, who knows what discoveries will be next?

WHAT IF?

What if
someday
I could spy

a brand-new planet
whizzing by?

Would aliens
reside there, too?

If they did,
what would they do?

Lasso asteroids
for fun?

Take school field trips
round their sun?

Play space kickball
with six feet?

Eat only veggies
or just meat?

What if
aliens
spied on me?

Would they like
all that
they see?

For Owen.
The sky is *not* the limit!
—A.E.S.

As always, for Lesly, Clare and Ian.
—S.S.

With special thanks for his expert advice to Professor Tim Paglione, Ph.D., Research Associate, American Museum of Natural History; Coordinator of Astronomy, Department of Earth and Physical Sciences, York College, City University of New York.

THIS IS A BORZOI BOOK PUBLISHED BY ALFRED A. KNOPF

Text copyright © 2012 by Amy E. Sklansky
Jacket art and interior illustrations copyright © 2012 by Stacey Schuett
All rights reserved. Published in the United States by Alfred A. Knopf, an imprint of Random House Children's Books,
a division of Random House, Inc., New York.
Knopf, Borzoi Books, and the colophon are registered trademarks of Random House, Inc.

Visit us on the Web! randomhouse.com/kids
Educators and librarians, for a variety of teaching tools, visit us at randomhouse.com/teachers

Library of Congress Cataloging-in-Publication Data is available upon request.

ISBN 978-0-375-86459-9 (trade) — ISBN 978-0-375-96459-6 (lib. bdg.)

The illustrations in this book were created using digital images and gouache.
MANUFACTURED IN MALAYSIA
February 2012   10 9 8 7 6 5 4 3 2 1   First Edition
Random House Children's Books supports the First Amendment and celebrates the right to read.